STORY SPINNER

Kate A. Rezvani

Kate A. Rezvani

Learning Circle Publishing Co.
Copyright © 1994
All rights reserved.

Story Spinner/by Kate A. Rezvani

ISBN 09641318-4-6
CIP 94-096237

Printed in the U.S.A.

Learning Circle Publishing Company
16212 Bothell Way S.E., Suite F162
Mill Creek, Washington 98012-1219
(206) 742-2994

Preface

I don't like writing outlines but I love writing stories. It's like having to get past all the thorns of a blackberry bush to reach that one delicious ripe berry. Notice all the best tasting ones are up high and in the center. I knew I had to quit indulging my negative feelings about outlining and plotting if I was to ever finish writing anything. Besides, my file labeled "Story Ideas" was imploding. My solution was to list all the elements of creative writing and most of the variables within each element. For example, with characterization there is eye color, body type, motives, personality traits, etc... Of course the variables for themes and plot twists are extensive so I offer you the best.

As for plotting, I took special pleasure in making it fun and easy by creating a chart on which cards could be moved around. It won't torment me any more.

Organizing all of the elements and variables wasn't enough; my whimsical side romped around me, yapping, "Make it fun! MAKE IT FUN!" I knew I had better oblige if I ever wanted another creative thought, so that's where the spinner fits in.

So you see, this approach to creative writing was a conspiracy executed by the two halves of my brain, my partners in crime, one my logical organized self, the other my irrepressible fun-loving creative one. I put up with both of them because they never get to enjoy the taste of a sun ripened blackberry like I do.

Author Biography

My first book was a cook book written for my Mom. The font looked like spider tracks on sand. The binding was made of dinosaur Band-Aids. I was five years old. It was illegible (which explains why she never used the chocolate chip cookie recipe I put three stars by). In any case, I learned writing gave me praise if not cookies.

Then in 4th grade I had an assignment to write about our school. I wrote about how the new landscaping around the school was ugly and probably cost so much our tuition would rise. The teacher gave my poem to the principal who tore it up in my face yelling, "Don't expect to have anything in the year book missy." I learned that writing brought me drama. **That** was the encouragement I needed to become a professional writer.

So far I've overeducated myself, traveled extensively and enjoyed the people around me. I'm married and we are raising a delightful two year old boy. We live fifteen miles north of Seattle on two soggy acres overrun by slugs.

Post Script: Someone told me ducks like to eat slugs so I got some ducks. It's true they do eat the slugs. Now I just have to stop the ducks from eating my husband's cucumber plants.

Introduction

How to use this Tool Book

The method *Story Spinner* uses to outline a story is explained below:

A spinner has been attached to a piece of clear plastic. Place this over each circle and spin the arrow. Look through the plastic to read the answer. To develop your story outline you sometimes spin this arrow; other times you answer a question (A to U) written in the text.

On the form titled Story Outline Form you write your answers. After certain sections on the Story Outline Form have been filled in you compile and summarize all the answers into sentences. Later these sentences can be used in your first draft.

Review:
• Spin the arrow over each circle.
• Answer the questions presented in the text.
• Transfer answers to the Story Outline Form.

The *Story Spinner* uses a third method to help you create an outline for a story; and in particular, with your plotting efforts. This method entails the use of scene and sequel cards, which are to be filled in by you and placed over the Plotting Chart. Using cards makes it possible for you to rearrange the chronological order of your plot.

After you've used the *Story Spinner* you will have your outline and plot finished. The next step is to read through the Check List. One by one it lists the important points which you, as the writer, need to address.

Review:
• Fill in the Scene and Sequel Cards.
• Place them over the Plotting Chart.
• Read through the Check List.

The text of this book provides definitions, explanations, examples and tips for better creative writing. After reading the text and following the procedures listed, its time to start writing. Refer to your Story Outline Form and the Plotting Chart any time you want. When your first draft is done go through the Check List once more.

Review:
• Read the text and follow the procedures.
• Write your story.
• Use the Check List.

The spinner is in the pocket on the inside of the back cover. Copies of the Story Outline Form, the Scene and Sequel Cards and the Check List are at the back of the book. They are perforated and reproducible. The Plotting Chart is also perforated so you can take it out of the book to place the scene and sequel cards on it.

The first time you use the *Story Spinner* you will need more time. Thereafter you will be able to outline stories rapidly. Using this book will allow you to put more of your time into the actual writing of your work.

Characterization

Physical Description

Readers like to know how the main characters look and something about their background.

The first step in creating a personal history for your main character is creating a physical description.

Spin the arrow over the first circle and write your answer on the Story Outline Form. Continue with the other circles on this page and the next. When you're finished combine your answers by writing them in a sentence. Space is provided on the Story Outline Form.

Note

If you want, include skin color, the shape of his/her face, and any birth marks.

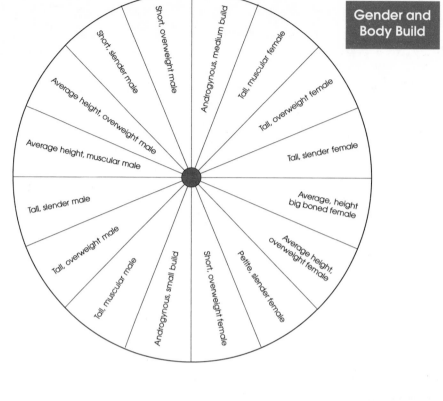

Gender and Body Build

- Short, overweight male
- Short, slender male
- Average height, overweight male
- Average height, muscular male
- Tall, slender male
- Tall, overweight male
- Tall, muscular male
- Androgynous, small build
- Short, overweight female
- Petite, slender female
- Average height, overweight female
- Average, height big boned female
- Tall, slender female
- Tall, overweight female
- Tall, muscular female
- Androgynous, medium build

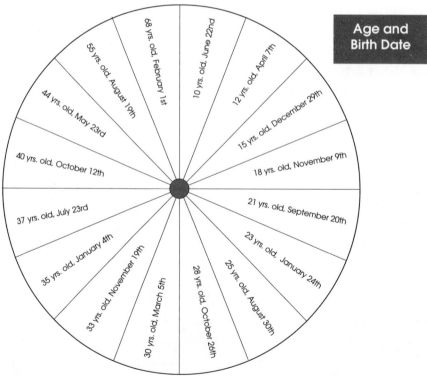

Age and Birth Date

- 68 yrs. old, February 1st
- 10 yrs. old, June 22nd
- 12 yrs. old, April 7th
- 15 yrs. old, December 29th
- 18 yrs. old, November 9th
- 21 yrs. old, September 20th
- 23 yrs. old, January 24th
- 25 yrs. old, August 30th
- 28 yrs. old, October 26th
- 30 yrs. old, March 5th
- 33 yrs. old, November 19th
- 35 yrs. old, January 4th
- 37 yrs. old, July 23rd
- 40 yrs. old, October 12th
- 44 yrs. old, May 23rd
- 55 yrs. old, August 19th

Building your central character, or protagonist, requires that you know him or her better than your readers. Some facts may never enter directly into your story but you should still create a complete personal history for this individual.

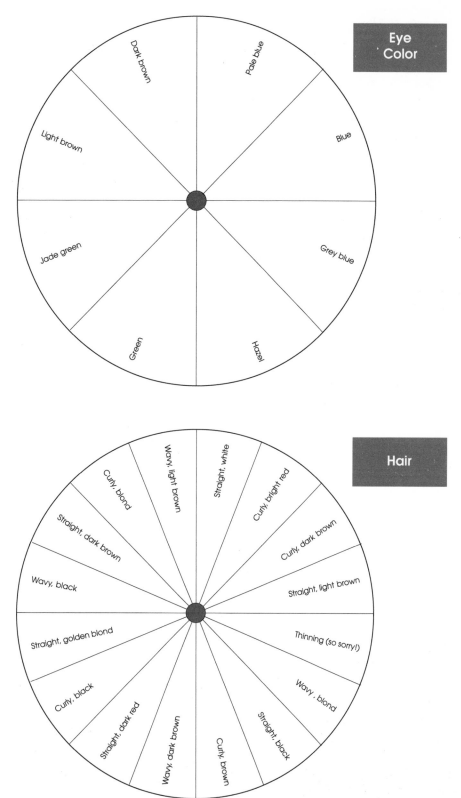

Eye Color

Dark brown
Pale blue
Light brown
Blue
Jade green
Grey blue
Green
Hazel

Hair

Wavy, light brown
Straight, white
Curly, blond
Curly, bright red
Straight, dark brown
Curly, dark brown
Wavy, black
Straight, light brown
Straight, golden blond
Thinning (so sorry!)
Curly, black
Wavy, blond
Straight, dark red
Straight, black
Wavy, dark brown
Curly, brown

Characterization
Continued

Personality

The personal habits of your character include mannerisms, routines, quirks and facial expressions which are unique to him or her. This circle lists some of the categories in which you can make up a behavior for your character.

Example:
Phobia: "Checks outside the window before sleeping at night."

Spin until you have two different habits. Write in sentence form what those habits are.

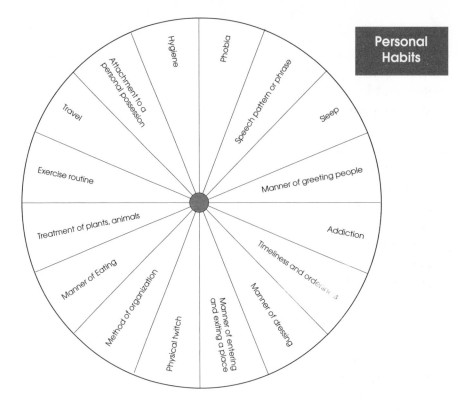

Personal Habits

Hygiene
Phobia
Attachment to a personal possession
Speech pattern or phrase
Travel
Sleep
Exercise routine
Manner of greeting people
Treatment of plants, animals
Addiction
Manner of Eating
Timeliness and orderliness
Method of organization
Manner of dressing
Physical twitch
Manner of entering and exiting a place

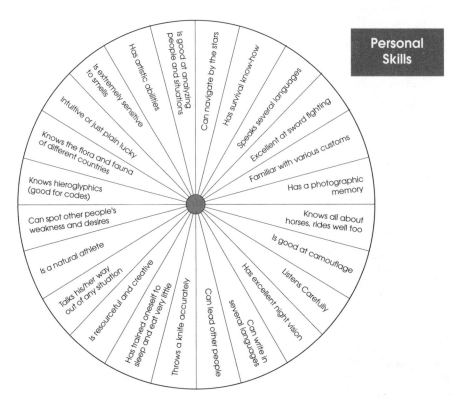

Personal Skills

Is good at analyzing people and situations
Has artistic abilities
Can navigate by the stars
Has survival know-how
Is extremely sensitive to smells
Speaks several languages
Intuitive or just plain lucky
Excellent at sword fighting
Knows the flora and fauna of different countries
Familiar with various customs
Knows hieroglyphics (good for codes)
Has a photographic memory
Can spot other people's weakness and desires
Knows all about horses, rides well too
Is a natural athlete
Is good at camouflage
Talks his/her way out of any situation
Listens Carefully
Is resourceful and creative
Has excellent night vision
Has trained oneself to sleep and eat very little
Can write in several languages
Throws a knife accurately
Can lead other people

4

When writing about a character's traits avoid adjectives. Use words that **demonstrate** the traits instead. For instance, if you spun the arrow and got "Clumsy and Helpful" try to bring these abstract ideas into concrete images. Instead of writing, "He is helpful," convey this trait with an action: He carried in all the groceries; with dialogue, "Let me carry these for you."

The protagonist should be everyone's hero/heroine. He/she should be the most active, admirable, vivid and highly motivated character in your story. Make the protagonist someone your readers can sympathize with, but don't ever let them pity your hero or heroine.

When you write your protagonist character profile keep in mind their main motive.

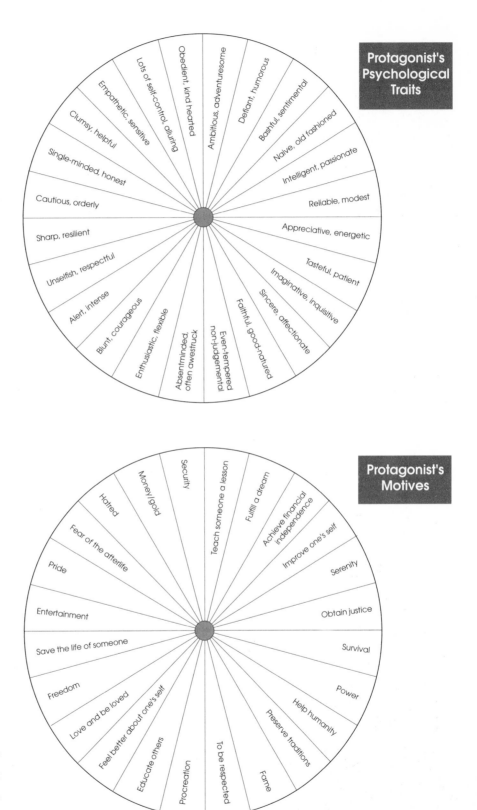

Occupation

Astronomer
Farmer
Cook
Teacher
Con Artist
Undertaker
Landlord
Banker
Hunter
Candlemaker
Carpenter
Advisory Consultant
Builder
Singer
Artist
Veterinarian
Healer/Physician
Thief
Seamstress/Tailor
Musician
Monarch
Herbalist
Scribe/Secretary
Blacksmith

Background

Select either circle to determine the birthplace of your character and where he or she grew up. It's okay if its the same place but spin again if you want it to be different. The circles on this page list cities and these on page 19 list towns. If you want your protagonist to have a rural background name the city or town nearest where they live. You can also make up a city or town and set it on an island, seacoast or in a valley. Finally, decide what type of dwelling they live in; an estate; a house they own, rent, or share with others; a boat; a shack; a palace, etc. Transfer your answers to the Story Outline Form.

Note

Choose one Socio-Economic class from which your character came: Poverty, working class, middle class, upper middle class, or wealthy.

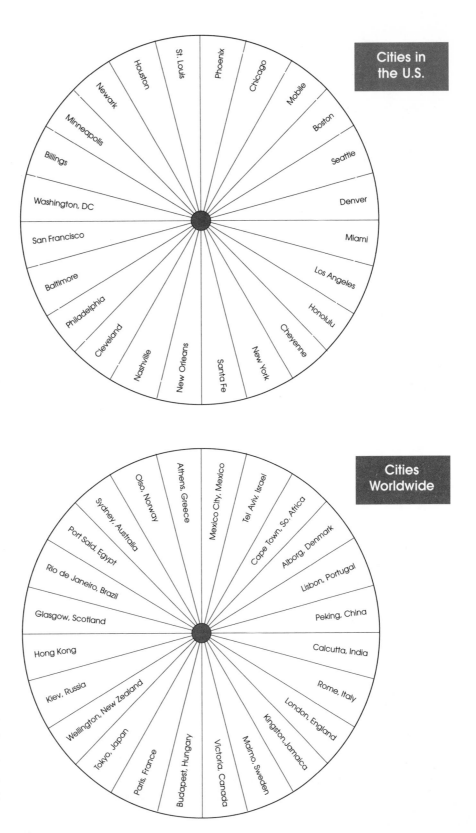

Cities in the U.S.

St. Louis, Phoenix, Chicago, Mobile, Boston, Seattle, Denver, Miami, Los Angeles, Honolulu, Cheyenne, New York, Santa Fe, New Orleans, Nashville, Cleveland, Philadelphia, Baltimore, San Francisco, Washington, DC, Billings, Minneapolis, Newark, Houston

Cities Worldwide

Athens, Greece; Oslo, Norway; Sydney, Australia; Port Said, Egypt; Rio de Janeiro, Brazil; Glasgow, Scotland; Hong Kong; Kiev, Russia; Wellington, New Zealand; Tokyo, Japan; Paris, France; Budapest, Hungary; Victoria, Canada; Malmo, Sweden; Kingston, Jamaica; London, England; Rome, Italy; Calcutta, India; Peking, China; Lisbon, Portugal; Alborg, Denmark; Cape Town, So. Africa; Tel Aviv, Israel; Mexico City, Mexico

Themes

Every story should have at least one central theme. Themes are ideas expressed through literature. They are assertions or statements about values people have and how they view those values.

Ask yourself how the many elements of writing, the characters, action, setting, dialog, structure, etc., be applied to this particular theme? Symbolism, imagery, implications and contradictions can supplement these elements and be interwoven into your story as you write. In other words, be subtle as you express the theme of your story. Let these different elements of writing do the job for you. Remember, people don't like to be lectured.

On these two pages are some of the many themes in life. Spin the arrow over either circle or think about your own life or someone you know for ideas.

Personal, Religious, Spiritual

Idleness is punishable by death

Show good judgement by not judging others

Some things/people are worth the price

Consider what holes others have fallen into

Overcoming problems created in childhood

Independence and dependence

Consolation in misfortune

Communication between family or friends

Running away from problems

Integrity in the face of corruption

Allow no mediocrity, live boldly

Regaining self-respect

Loneliness

Only bend where you know you won't break

No one can make laws regarding love-love is a law onto itself

Sincerity/being true to oneself

Where expectation goes disappointment follows

Rigidity sucks the joy out of life

It is permissible to let the heart dupe the mind

Experience precedes knowledge

Adopt a view that lets you dread death no more than your bed

Hard work can be rewarded

Selfishness leads to loss of self

The composition of life comes from our thoughts

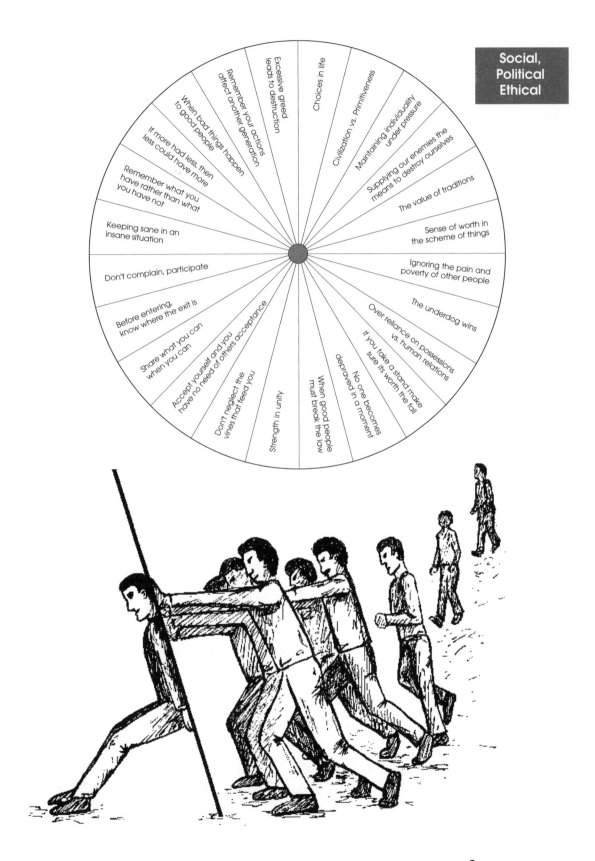

Social, Political Ethical

Choices in life
Civilization vs. Primitiveness
Maintaining individuality under pressure
Supplying our enemies the means to destroy ourselves
The value of traditions
Sense of worth in the scheme of things
Ignoring the pain and poverty of other people
The underdog wins
Over reliance on possessions vs. human relations
If you take a stand make sure its worth the fall
No one becomes depraved in a moment
When good people must break the law
Strength in unity
Don't neglect the vines that feed you
Accept yourself and you have no need of others acceptance
Share what you can when you can
Before entering, know where the exit is
Don't complain, participate
Keeping sane in an insane situation
Remember what you have rather than what you have not
If more had less, then less could have more
When bad things happen to good people
Remember your actions affect another generation
Excessive greed leads to destruction

Structure

Theme Conveyance

There are six ways themes can be conveyed. Later, when you write your story keep them in mind. The first one is recommended.

1. The theme becomes an inseparable part of the entire work's impression.
2. A character who stands for an idea; his/her actions reflect his/her values.
3. Figurative language which represents and reinforces ideas.

4. The characters can make dramatic statements to express their views and values.
5. First person speaker or narrator who expresses personal ideas.
6. The author can make direct statements expressing ideas.

Character Viewpoint

After reading through the following three choices pick one viewpoint to start with. Write it down on your Story Outline Form.

1. First Person, (I and me). In this case, the speaker may have total understanding; may have no understanding at all; or may have an incorrect or partial understanding.
2. Second Person, (you). This is when the speaker knows more about a character's actions than he/she does him/herself.

3. Third Person, (she, he, it, they). Here, the speaker is not involved in the action and just reports what the speeches and actions of others are. The thoughts and feelings of characters can be told only as dialogue. Or, the speaker focuses on one major character and reports everything. Or lastly, the speaker is 'omniscient', knows and reports everything by all characters.

Time Frame

What is the time frame or the duration of your story going to be? Is it three days, one month or several months? You need to decide early on. Write your decision on the Story Outline Form now.

Each viewpoint creates its own impact on how your story will sustain interest. Sometimes by switching viewpoints within a story it helps create more suspense.

10

Story Types

Essentially there are three types of stories. A story can combine more than one type. All, however, start with a person who vaguely or fully realizes they are LACKING something.

1. One type of story requires that a **Decision** be made. This is when the protagonist finally reaches a point where a hard decision must be made. It is a decision that will have a life changing affect.

2. In the story of **Conflict** the protagonist has a specific goal that must be attained in order to be happy. Someone or something is opposing him/her, the struggle lasts until there is a final confrontation and one wins, one loses.

3. The **Discovery** tale is considered the most difficult to write because it is subtle and depends on style and tone. Here the protagonist struggles to reach some kind of understanding.

Story Question

In each story there should be one thing reader's worry about excessively. They've just got to learn how it turns out for the protagonist. This worry is the story question which you as the writer must ask and then answer for your readers. You cannot have a story without a story question. In addition, you must demonstrate that this story question is essential to the protagonist's fulfillment. A clear concise story question will help direct your focus as you write.

The **beginning** of a story should set up the story question, the **middle** should continue it, intensifying the audience's worry. The **ending** must answer this question. The ending should provide a satisfying outcome for the characters by clearly and definitively answering the story question. Don't be vague or unclear about the story question otherwise the reader won't worry about anything in particular. If there's no worry there's no interest and your story gets put down. End of story... Period!

The story question can be answered in a number of ways. Here are three examples.

1. A change in mood or tone.
2. A simple yes or no.
3. A solution to a puzzle.

Whatever method you choose, be sure the answer to the story question is clear.

Obstacles

Below are listed some examples of types of obstacles your protagonist may have to overcome. Spin the arrow in the circle and find the corresponding number in the list. Pick one variance (a, b or c).

1. Age: a) Too young or old to be capable. b) Someone is insisting that the protagonist is not the right age.

2. Gender Discrimination: a) Someone is maintaining that the protagonist is not of the appropriate gender for that goal or activity. b) Social customs state that the protagonist is not of the appropriate gender for that goal or activity. c) Nature herself dictates that the protagonist is not of the appropriate gender for that goal or activity.

3. Poor Health: Short/long term debilitating disease or syndrome.

4. Physically incapable, differently abled: a) Since birth. b) Due to disease. c) From an accident.

5. Conditioned Psychologically: a) Because of how one was socialized. b) Due to one's individual beliefs or perspective from life experiences.

6. Personal Faults: a) Caused by a deed from one's past b) All-prevailing feelings or behavior for which no underlying cause is evident.

7. Finances: a) Too little money. b) Over-dependence on money for one's self-esteem. c) One's existence revolves

Structure
Continued

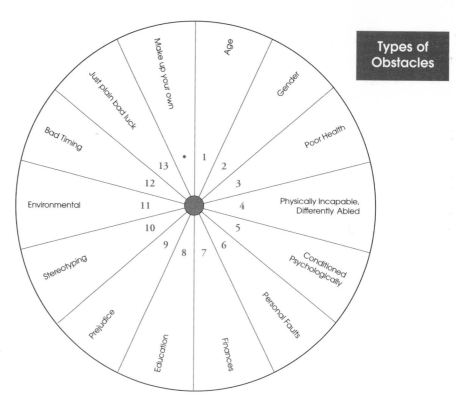

around the pursuit of money.

8. Education: a) Too little. b) Too much. c) The wrong kind.

9. Prejudice: a) By an individual against one because of race, ethnic origin, appearance, religion or beliefs. b) by a society or group because of race, ethnic origin, appearance, religion or beliefs.

10. Stereotyping: a) By another person because of race, ethnic, origin, appearance, religion or beliefs. b) by a society or group because of race, ethnic origin, appearance, religion or beliefs.

11. Environmental obstacles which are either man-made or natural.

12. Bad timing.

13. Just plain bad luck.

Consider the theme, the story type, the obstacle and the protagonist's motive while trying to answer questions A-C. Make your answers brief but complete.

A. What is the protagonist wanting or lacking?

B. Why is it vital for the protagonist to:
1) Come to a decision? (Decision story type).
2) Reach his/her goals? (Conflict).
3) Find new insight? (Discovery).

C. What is the main obstacle preventing the protagonist from achieving that goal?

Genre

If you haven't already decided on a genre, spin the arrow over the title page and let chance decide for you. Some of the types of genre stories are listed on this page and on the next two. Spin the arrow over the circle for the genre you picked.

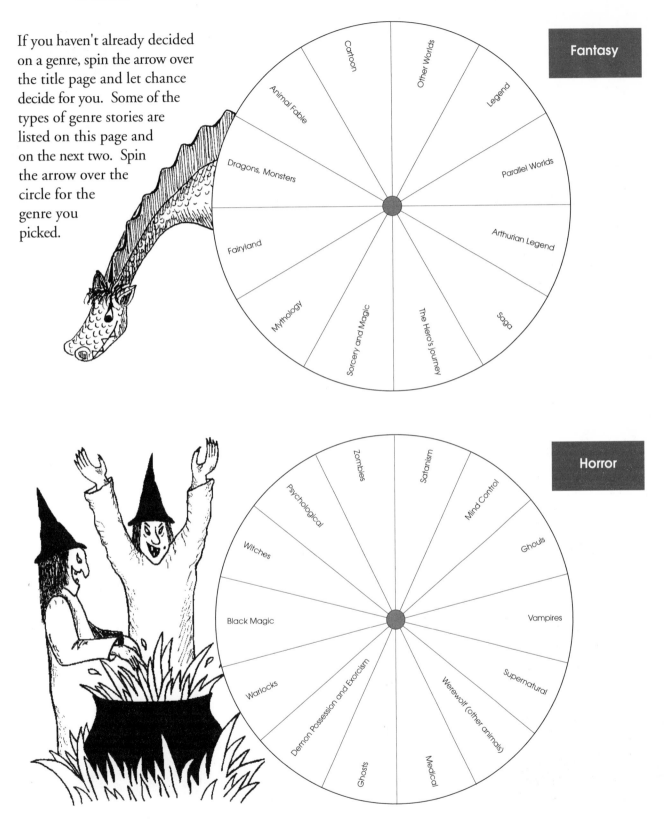

Fantasy

Cartoon
Other Worlds
Legend
Animal Fable
Parallel Worlds
Dragons, Monsters
Arthurian Legend
Fairyland
Saga
Mythology
Sorcery and Magic
The Hero's Journey

Horror

Zombies
Satanism
Psychological
Mind Control
Witches
Ghouls
Black Magic
Vampires
Warlocks
Supernatural
Demon Possession and Exorcism
Werewolf (other animals)
Ghosts
Medical

Structure
Continued

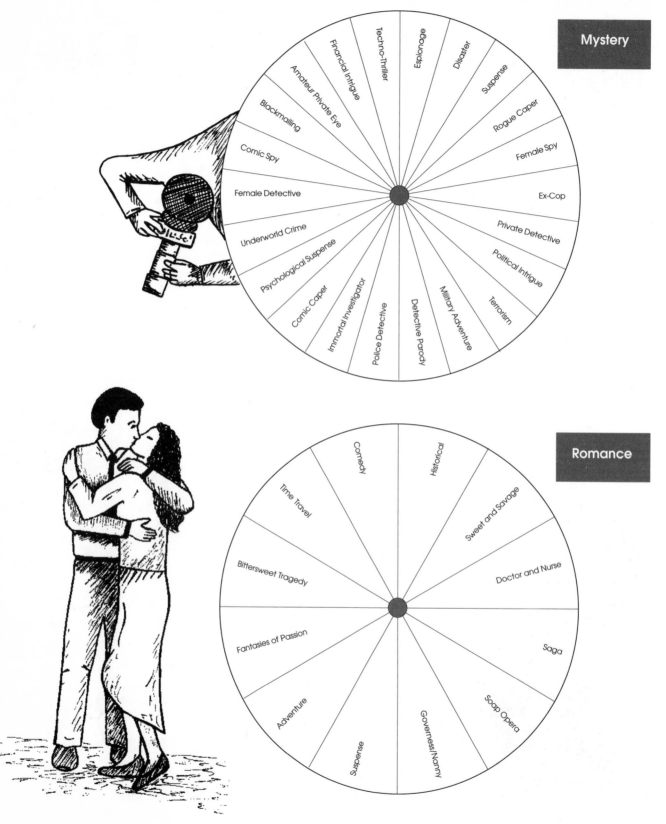

Mystery

- Techno-Thriller
- Espionage
- Financial Intrigue
- Disaster
- Amateur Private Eye
- Suspense
- Blackmailing
- Rogue Caper
- Comic Spy
- Female Spy
- Female Detective
- Ex-Cop
- Underworld Crime
- Private Detective
- Psychological Suspense
- Political Intrigue
- Comic Caper
- Terrorism
- Immortal Investigator
- Military Adventure
- Police Detective
- Detective Parody

Romance

- Comedy
- Historical
- Time Travel
- Sweet and Savage
- Bittersweet Tragedy
- Doctor and Nurse
- Fantasies of Passion
- Saga
- Adventure
- Soap Opera
- Suspense
- Governess/Nanny

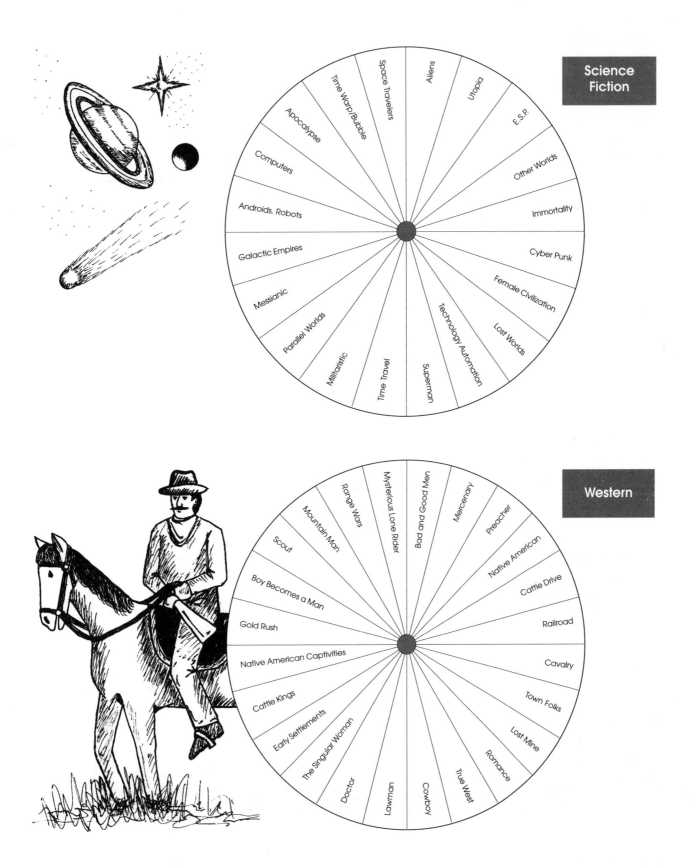

Science Fiction

Space Travelers · Aliens · Utopia · E.S.P. · Other Worlds · Immortality · Cyber Punk · Female Civilization · Lost Worlds · Technology Automation · Superman · Time Travel · Militaristic · Parallel Worlds · Messianic · Galactic Empires · Androids, Robots · Computers · Apocalypse · Time Warp/Bubble

Western

Mysterious Lone Rider · Bad and Good Men · Mercenary · Preacher · Native American · Cattle Drive · Railroad · Cavalry · Town Folks · Lost Mine · Romance · True West · Cowboy · Lawman · Doctor · The Singular Woman · Early Settlements · Cattle Kings · Native American Captivities · Gold Rush · Boy Becomes a Man · Scout · Mountain Man · Range Wars

Antagonist

Definition

The antagonist is the person or element who opposes the protagonist. Almost anything can be an antagonist: natural forces; such as bad weather, difficult terrain or animals; supernatural forces like ghouls and demons; or a group of people. On page 12 is a list of obstacles. Some could apply to the antagonist.

D. If the antagonist is not a human being, what is the antagonist? Put your answer on the Story Outline Form.

If your antagonist is not a person try personifying "it" once or twice when you write your story.

Physical Description

If you have elected to have your antagonist be a person it's best if you have a clear image of this character. Go through the characterization section on pages 2-7. Don't spin the arrow over the circles on page 5 labeled Protagonist's Psychological Traits and Protagonist's Motive. The antagonist's motive will be to stop the protagonist from achieving that goal.

In order to complete "E" on the Story Outline Form, spin the arrow until you get two different traits.

E. What are the negative psychological traits of the antagonist?

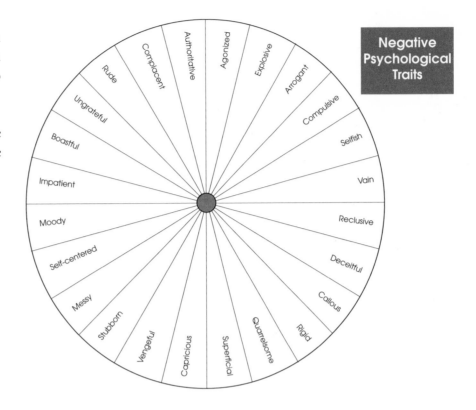

Negative Psychological Traits

Authoritative
Complacent
Rude
Ungrateful
Boastful
Impatient
Moody
Self-centered
Messy
Stubborn
Vengeful
Capricious
Superficial
Quarrelsome
Rigid
Callous
Deceitful
Reclusive
Vain
Selfish
Compulsive
Arrogant
Explosive
Agonized

F. Assign one human characteristic to your antagonist. Be aware that the antagonist doesn't always have to inspire hatred in the audience. Sometimes the antagonist is also a victim. Sometimes he or she is just doing what must be done. Make the antagonist a little human no matter how evil.

G. If you selected a **Decision Story Type** then why is it essential to the antagonist's to persuade the protagonist to make the wrong decision?

If you selected a **Conflict Story Type** then why is it essential to the antagonist to oppose the protagonist?

If you selected a **Discovery Story Type** then why is it essential to the antagonist to keep the protagonist from the insight or discovery that might give him/her happiness?

H. The antagonist must have a plan and some underlying logic. Consider how the antagonist might stop the protagonist. What is the antagonist's plan to thwart the protagonist's attempt to reach the desired goal?

Other Characters

Relationship to Protagonist

Usually stories have two to five characters including the protagonist and antagonist. The role and/or relationship of these other characters to the protagonist needs to be identified. Supportive and secondary characters can be any one of the people in the circle to the right. They can also be romantic interests, victims, sidekicks or even business partners. Frequently a supportive character is a spouse, whereas a secondary character usually performs a job or has some function in the protagonist's life.

Decide for yourself or spin the arrow to determine what relationship the antagonist and the other characters have with the protagonist.

I. What is the antagonist's relationship to the protagonist?

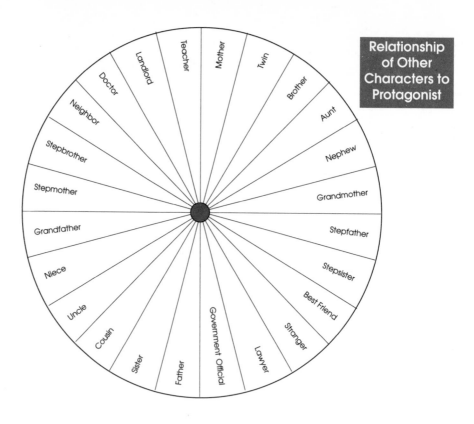

Relationship of Other Characters to Protagonist

Teacher, Mother, Twin, Brother, Aunt, Nephew, Grandmother, Stepfather, Stepsister, Best Friend, Stranger, Lawyer, Government Official, Father, Sister, Cousin, Uncle, Niece, Grandfather, Stepmother, Stepbrother, Neighbor, Doctor, Landlord

Development of Other Characters

Each character in a story can be described as flat or round. A flat character doesn't change his or her opinions, world view or feelings from the start of the story to the end. A round character will change views, adapt, have realizations, etc. Rarely is the protagonist a flat character. You should decide what each character will be, flat or round.

J. Is the antagonist a flat or round character?

Answer for both Supportive and Secondary Characters:

K. If you decided on a round character: What change does the character go through by the end of the story?

L. What is a major trait and minor trait this character has?

M. How will this character help and hinder the protagonist consciously or unconsciously?

18

Setting

The setting should imediately establish the environment and tone of your story. Settings may change depending on the scene. Try to mix into your setting some symbolism or have some kind of metaphor.

Question how the setting interacts with the characters. Does it uplift them, adversely affect them or maybe change with them? Does it affect their routine, behavior, habits, customs and basic survival? Consider all of these points when creating a setting.

To find out where the story takes place choose from one of the circles here or from page 7. Then continue spinning the arrow over the remaining circles on the next few pages to establish your story setting.

Afterwards combine the answers into one paragraph. Space is provided on the Story Outline Form.

Tip

Your writing style should create the tone and mood for each setting.

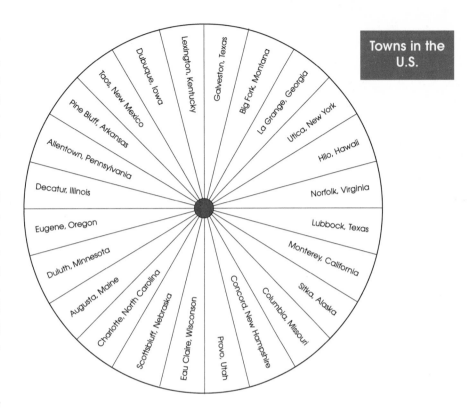

Towns in the U.S.

Lexington, Kentucky
Dubuque, Iowa
Taos, New Mexico
Pine Bluff, Arkansas
Allentown, Pennsylvania
Decatur, Illinois
Eugene, Oregon
Duluth, Minnesota
Augusta, Maine
Charlotte, North Carolina
Scottsbluff, Nebraska
Eau Claire, Wisconson
Provo, Utah
Concord, New Hampshire
Columbia, Missouri
Sitka, Alaska
Monterey, California
Lubbock, Texas
Norfolk, Virginia
Hilo, Hawaii
Utica, New York
La Grange, Georgia
Big Fork, Montana
Galveston, Texas

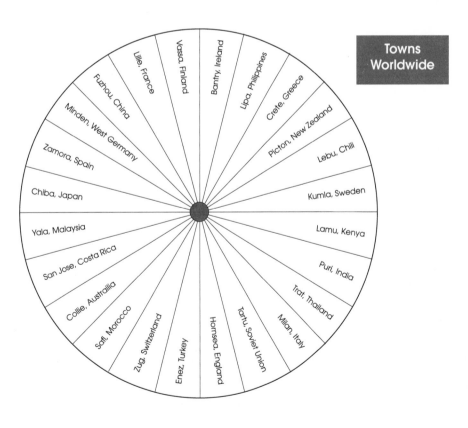

Towns Worldwide

Vassa, Finland
Lille, France
Fuzhou, China
Minden, West Germany
Zamora, Spain
Chiba, Japan
Yala, Malaysia
San Jose, Costa Rica
Collie, Australlia
Sofi, Morocco
Zug, Switzerland
Enez, Turkey
Hornsea, England
Tartu, Soviet Union
Milan, Italy
Trat, Thailand
Puri, India
Lamu, Kenya
Kumla, Sweden
Lebu, Chili
Picton, New Zealand
Crete, Greece
Lipa, Phillippines
Bantry, Ireland

Setting

Continued

Those who selected Western for their genre will need to spin again if the arrow lands on a space with a dot.

It's essential that you have a basic knowledge of the era and the country where your story takes place. The food, language, clothing, architecture, currency, music, recreation, transportation, etc., may require research.

A good starting point for any research you have to do are the following reference books at your local library:

-Culturegram (series)
-The Statesman's Yearbook
-The Encyclopedia of Anthropology
-An Encyclopedia of World History
-World Civilizations
-International Encyclopedia of Social Sciences
-Cambridge Encyclopedia of Languages
-Folk and Festival Costumes of the World
-Historical Encyclopedia of World Coins
-The International Encyclopedia of Music
-A Dictionary of Surnames

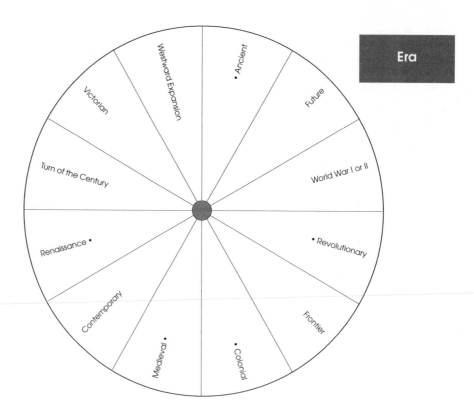

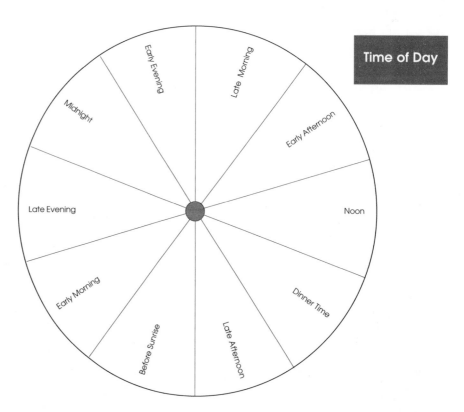

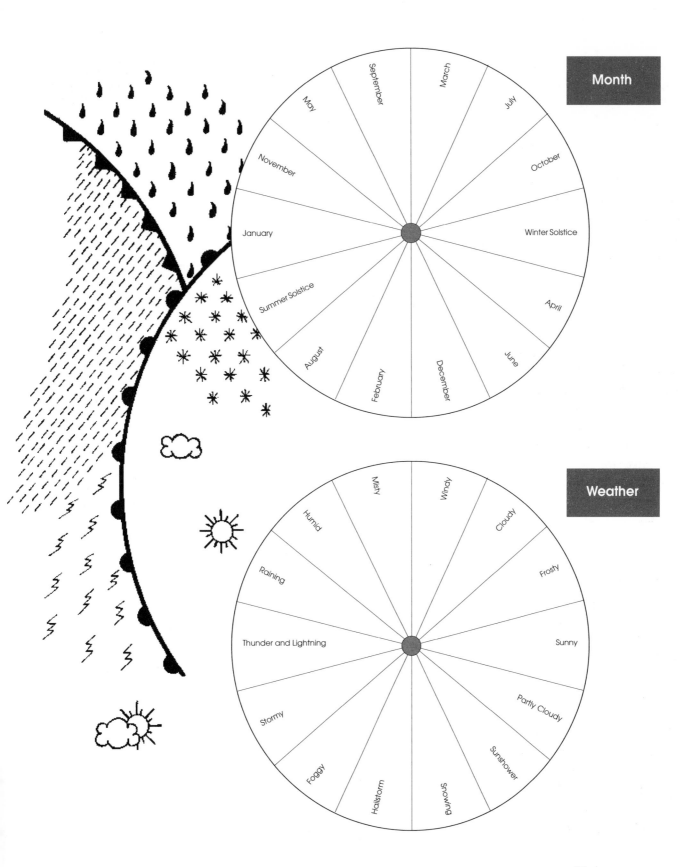

Opening Scene

An opening scene should immediately grab the attention of the reader. To keep your reader's interest you should use dramatic action, dialogue and action verbs from the start. Stay away from too many descriptive passages. Do not rely on the inner thoughts of characters to describe events.

The opening scene needs to be intergrated with the setting you choose for the beginning. The beginning of your story should introduce the main characters and establish the setting. Part of the setting includes mood and atmosphere which are revealed through lighting, emotions, thoughts, colors, smells and sounds. Spin the arrow over the next three circles and put your answers on the Story Outline Form.

Whether it's a public place or private; busy or solitary; in natural surroundings or in a man-made structure the location also sets the mood. Decide what is most constructive in creating the overall effect you desire.

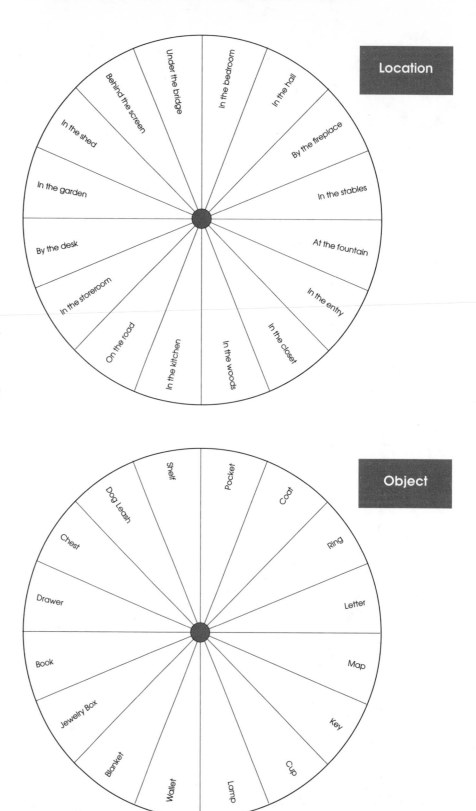

Location

Under the bridge
In the bedroom
In the hall
Behind the screen
By the fireplace
In the shed
In the stables
In the garden
At the fountain
By the desk
In the entry
In the storeroom
In the closet
On the road
In the kitchen
In the woods

Object

Shelf
Pocket
Coat
Dog Leash
Ring
Chest
Letter
Drawer
Map
Book
Key
Jewelry Box
Cup
Blanket
Lamp
Wallet

Action
Verbs

Jumps over
Rushes in
Fiddles with
Sits down
Peeks through
Hides behind
Runs by
Walks over to
Knocks over
Lifts up
Reaches around
Pushes aside
Falls over
Pulls down
Throws away
Carries to

23

N. Below is a list of how the protagonist's personality and character can be revealed in a story. Decide on one now in preparation for organizing your opening scene.

1. What the protagonist's thoughts are;
2. What the protagonist says;
3. What the protagonist does;
4. What the author says; about them, speaking as a storyteller or observer;

5. What other characters say about them.

For an opening scene the last method, #5, is highly recommended. Having two people talk about a third person usually gets people's attention.

O. Here are the possible combinations of two main characters in conversation: Choose one for your opening scene.

Protagonist - Antagonist
Antagonist - Supportive
Antagonist - Secondary
Supportive - Secondary
Protagonist - Supportive
Protagonist - Secondary

The first combination should be used in the climax of your last scene. Recommended for some of the other scene climaxes, too.

Listed to the right are some phrases as suggestions for opening lines. Insert these examples in your story or use them as a springboard in making up your own phrases. A fun and helpful method to collect authentic sounding bits of dialogue is to carry a stack of 3x5 cards and record conversations verbatim as you sit in the mall, at a cafe, on the bus, etc. Usually, well written dialogue goes unnoticed whereas artificial, forced dialogue doesn't. Always read the conversations you write out loud to yourself to determine if you have caught the rhythm of speech. Avoid using slang.

Fantasy
"You promise not to tell?"
"Where will this take me?"
"I wonder why this is..."
"You need to find the..."

Horror
"Who could have done this?"
"Are you okay?"
"It's too bad it has to end this way."
"What else did they uncover?"

Mystery
"It must be somewhere"
"Who else was there?"
"We must hurry or else..."
"She's got to be here somewhere."

Romance
"He couldn't stop her."
"How could you!"
"Well, he'll just have to accept it."
"It's so unfair! Where will I go?"

Science-Fiction
"I wonder how this works?"
"This is some kind of mistake."
"How can we get out of here?"
"It has taken over control."

Western
"No matter how, one day, I'll..."
"Where are you going?"
"They're all against you now."
"Someone is following our trail."

Plotting

Essentially, to plot is to list in chronological order all the actions of characters. These actions must be based on plausible human motivations. They should also be the result of realistic and believable human responses. Plotting these actions and responses can be done by using scenes and sequels. There is one more thing to consider when plotting. In addition to listing all the actions of characters, include all the incidents that happen in the story.

Scene

A scene presents the goal and problem of the protagonist at that moment; then the conflict and resulting disaster because of his/her attempt at attaining that goal. Each scene must end in disaster, with greater and newer complications and obstacles arising each time until the ending scene. Examples of obstacles are listed on page 12. Think about your own life or people you know for ideas. **Conflict** causes doubt and tension which creates interest in your audience. The way to bring out conflict is by establishing the **complication** or obstacle and put the protagonist and antagonist together. This will cause a **crisis**, the point where tension and uncertainty is greatest. The crisis separates what just occurred from the start of the new direction or next decision taken by the protagonist. After the crisis, the **climax** comes, it is the logical conclusion of prior uncertainty and tension. Try to maintain this structural sequence of conflict, complication, crisis and climax. Keep repeating this sequence throughout your story.

Sequel

After each scene is a sequel. The sequel presents how the viewpoint character (usually protagonist) first **feels** about what just happened, then what he/she **thinks** about it, and finally what **decision** is made. The amount of time given to address these points can vary with each set. Normally a story has two scene/sequel sets in the beginning; four or five sets in the middle; and two sets in the ending.

The Ending

Most successful writers know the ending to their story before they write their first sentence. Try this approach if you haven't already. Think over the following questions and answer them now even if you change them later as your story unfolds. Remember, the ending is at the story's climax.

The climax can be some kind of dramatic action or the symbolic falling of a leaf, but it must be a logical conclusion of all the previous tension and uncertainty. After the climax, comes the final scene, you should resolve all loose ends to the satisfaction of the audience.

P. When will the story end?
Q. Who will be there?
R. Why?
S. Where will the ending scene take place?
T. What is going to happen?
U. What is the ending going to mean?

Spin the arrow over the circle to the right and write your answer and number on the Story Outline Form. Then find the corresponding number in the list of plot twists below and on the next page. Choose one variance (a,b,c...) for that number. This should be the intial plot twist you use while writing your story.

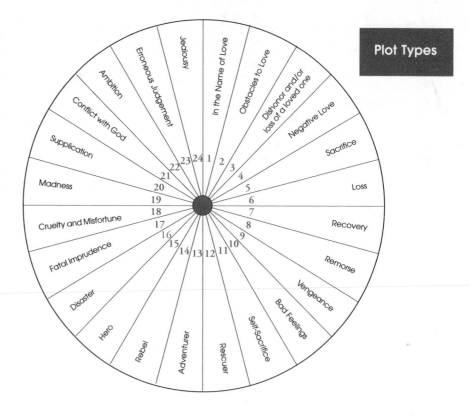

Plot Types

Plot Twists

1. In the Name of Love:
a) An adventure undertaken.
b) Sacrificing yourself or something you value for love or passionate love.
c) Unrequited love.
d) Rivalry between two wives. e) Abduction of a consenting woman.
f) Pursuit by others because of what one did for a loved one. g) Abandonment by lover or spouse.
h) Favorite or intimate being forgotten.
i) Two almost equal in status but only one is loved.

2. Obstacles to Love:
a) An enemy is loved.
b) Incompatibility.
c) Love itself. d) Relatives,
e) Previous engagement/ betrothal. f) Unequal fortune or social rank.
3. Dishonor or Loss of loved one.
4. Negative Love:
a) Adultery.
b) Murderous adultery.
c) Unwilling abduction-recapture without/with slaying the abductor.
d) Unknown, involuntary incest or adultery.

e) Mistaken jealousy.
f) Prejudice upon an entire sex because of the involvement with one of that sex.
5. Sacrifice: a) Of one's self to save loved ones.
b) Necessity of sacrificing loved ones.
6. Loss: a) Of children by parents.   b) Witness to death(s) one cannot stop.
c) Loss of loved ones through death or abduction, for example, ransom, slavery, or possession of.
7. Recovery of a long, lost loved one.

8. Remorse: a) For slaying an unrecognized kinsman/loved one.

9. Vengeance: a) Avenging the dishonor or attempted dishonor of a child or spouse, friend or family member. b) Avenging the slaying of a child or descendent, or a parent or ancestor. c) Taking revenge for the intentional robbing, spoliation or injury of a loved one or of one's property.

10. Bad Feelings: Enmity, rivalry, jealousy, betrayal and false accusation of a family member(s) or a loved one(s).

11. Self-Sacrifice: a) For an ideal. b) For one's people. c) For one's faith. d) Beliefs and values. e) Because gave one's word. f) For one's monarch or government.
g) Because of filial piety.

12. Rescuer: a) Appearance of a rescuer to the condemned just in time to save them. b) Rescuing family or friend(s). c) Search and rescue of a stranger.

13. Adventurer: a) Who takes adventurous expeditions. b) 'Professionally' pursues criminals. c) Carries off a desired person or object. d) Recaptures a desired person or object. e) Prepares for and partakes in combat or war.

14. Rebel: a) One who conspires against a tyrant individually. b) One who influences others to revolt.

15. Hero: a) One who challenges a superior force such as a: conqueror; monarch; powerful politician or businessman; evil person; someone with extra powers; rich. b) One who becomes a fugitive of justice and gains or does not gain popular support.

16. Disaster: a) Due to a natural catastrophe. b) A monarch being over thrown. c) Entire village/homeland destroyed. d) All of humanity affected. e) A defeat suffered in combat.

17. Fatal Imprudence:
a) Because one lacks prudence he/she causes others misfortune or death. b) And/or causes one's own misfortune, loss or dishonor.

18. Cruelty and Misfortune:
a) An innocent is despoiled by those who should protect. b) An innocent becomes a victim of ambitious intrigue. c) Some type of unjust punishment or enmity is suffered. d) An outrage is suffered. e) An ill-fated chance meeting.

19. Madness: a) Caused by heredity. b) Grief over loved ones. c) Inability to accept reality. d) Causing disgrace to self and/or others.
e) Unintentionally injuring or slaying others. f) Killing other people intentionally.

20. Supplication:
a) When one intervenes on behalf of a relative to another relative.
b) Begging the powerful on behalf of those dear to the supplicant. c) Fugitive(s) beseeching the powerful for help against their enemies.
d) Appeal for a refuge or a place to die. e) Charity besought by one who has been cast off by their own people whom they have disgraced. f) Seeking deliverance, pardon or healing. g) The surrender of a solicited relic.
h) Imploring assistance for the performance of a forbidden pious duty.

21. Conflict with God.

22. Ambition

23. Erroneous Judgement/False suspicions

24. Jealousy
a) Malicious rumors.
b) Traitor with a motive.
c) Suspicious type of mind.

Cut out eight of the scene cards and eight of the sequel cards. Consider everything you've done so far on your Story Outline Form. Begin filling in your scene and sequel cards. When you are done, place them on the Plotting Chart in the order you like most. Then begin writing your story. Remember to use the Check List after your first draft is completed. I wish you well in your endeavor and hope you had fun using this book.

Plotting Chart

Opening Scene: The opening scene should start at the moment of change in the protagonist's life where things will never again be the same. For example: a death occurs, a letter is received, a job is lost. Start the story as late into your story as you can.

Scene	Sequel

Beginning: The beginning of a story should introduce the main characters as well as establish the story question. Rely on dialogue and action to catch the reader's attention.

Scene	Sequel

Plotting Chart
Continued

Middle: The middle of the story perpetuates and progressively heightens the reader's worry about how the story question is answered. Throughout the middle of the story the protagonist demonstrates what he or she is willing to do to resolve problems or attain goals. Also the middle section of a story is used to portray the development of relationships.

Scene

Sequel

Scene

Sequel

Plotting Chart
Continued

Middle continued:

Scene

Sequel

Scene

Sequel

Plotting Chart
Continued

Final Climax: This part of a story should intensify the conflict. It should increase the anxiety of whether the protagonist does or doesn't get what he or she lacked . Clearly show the inevitable conclusion of the story question.

Scene	Sequel

Final Scene: The dramatic build up from the final climax should end here but nonetheless it must be exciting and/or emotionally satisfying. The ending resolves everything in the story.

Scene	Sequel

Scene

Goal:

Problem:

Conflict:

Disaster:

Sequel

Feel:

Think:

Decision:

Scene

Goal:

Problem:

Conflict:

Disaster:

Sequel

Feel:

Think:

Decision:

Scene

Goal:

Problem:

Conflict:

Disaster:

Sequel

Feel:

Think:

Decision:

Scene

Goal:

Problem:

Conflict:

Disaster:

Sequel

Feel:

Think:

Decision:

Scene

Goal:

Problem:

Conflict:

Disaster:

Sequel

Feel:

Think:

Decision:

Scene

Goal:

Problem:

Conflict:

Disaster:

Sequel

Feel:

Think:

Decision:

Scene

Goal:

Problem:

Conflict:

Disaster:

Sequel

Feel:

Think:

Decision:

Scene

Goal:

Problem:

Conflict:

Disaster:

Sequel

Feel:

Think:

Decision:

Scene

Goal:

Problem:

Conflict:

Disaster:

Sequel

Feel:

Think:

Decision:

Scene

Goal:

Problem:

Conflict:

Disaster:

Sequel

Feel:

Think:

Decision:

Scene

Goal:

Problem:

Conflict:

Disaster:

Sequel

Feel:

Think:

Decision:

Scene

Goal:

Problem:

Conflict:

Disaster:

Sequel

Feel:

Think:

Decision:

Story Outline Form

Characterization

Protagonist's Physical Description: Pages 2,3

Gender: _____ Body Build: _____ Age: _____

Date of Birth: _____ Eye Color: _____ Hair: _____

Write a physical description of your protagonist: _____

_____

_____

Protagonist's Personality: Pages 4-6

First Name: _____ Last Name: _____

Personal Habits 1) _____

Personal Habits 2) _____

Personal Skills: _____

Psychological Traits 1) _____

Psychological Traits 2) _____

Motive: _____

Occupation: _____

Protagonist's Background: Pages 7,19

Birthplace: _____ Grew Up: _____

Type of Dwelling: _____ Soc./Eco. Class: _____

Summarize the personality and background facts: _____

_____

_____

_____

Themes Pages 8,9

Central Theme: _____

Other themes you like: _____

Structure Pages 10,11

Method you want to use to convey the main theme: _____

_____

Primary Character Viewpoint: _____

Time Frame: _____ Story Type: _____

Reproducible

Structure

Continued Pages 11-15

State your Story Question: _____

_____

_____

How will the Story Question be answered: _____

_____

_____

_____

Main Obstacle: _____

Answers to Questions A-C:

A) _____

_____

B) _____

_____

C) _____

_____

Genre: _____ Genre Story Line: _____

Antagonist

D) If the antagonist is not human, what is the antagonist? _____

Antagonist's Physical Description: Pages 2,3

Gender: _____ Body Build: _____ Age: _____

Date of Birth: _____ Eye Color: _____ Hair: _____

Write a physical description of your antagonist: _____

_____

Antagonist's Personality and Background: Pages 4,6,7,17

First Name: _____ Last Name: _____

Personal Habit 1) _____

Personal Habit 2) _____

Personal Skills: _____

Occupation: _____

Birthplace: _____ Grew Up: _____

Type of Dwelling: _____ Soc./Eco. Class: _____

E) Negative Psychological Traits: 1) _____ 2) _____

Example sentence illustrating these traits: _____

_____

_____

_____

Antagonist

Continued Pages 16,17

F) Human Characteristic: _____

Example sentence illustrating this trait: _____

_____

Summarize these facts about the antagonist to create a character profile: _____

_____

_____

Antagonist's Plan: Pages 17,18

G) State why the antagonist must stop the protagonist:

_____

_____

_____

H) Describe the antagonist's plan: _____

_____

_____

I) The antagonist's relationship to the protagonist is: _____

J) Is the antagonist a flat or round character: _____

Other Characters

Supportive and Secondary Characters: Page 18

The role/relationship of the supportive character to the protagonist is: _____

Is the supportive character flat or round: _____

The role/relationship of the secondary character to the protagonist is: _____

Is the secondary character flat or round: _____

Answers to Questions K-M: Supportive Character

K) _____

_____

L) _____

_____

M) _____

Answers to Questions K-M: Secondary Character

K) _____

_____

L) _____

_____

M) _____

Setting Pages 19-21

The story will take place in: _____ Era: _____

Circle areas you will need to research:

Food   Language   Clothing   Architecture   Currency   Arts   Transportation

Time of Day: _____ Month: _____ Weather: _____

Opening Scene Pages 22-24

Location: _____ Object: _____ Action Verb: _____

Dialogue

N) The protagonist character will be revealed by: _____

_____

O) The opening scene will have the two following characters in conversation: _____

Setting and Opening Scene

Write in sentence format the setting and opening scene for your story by combining all your answers from above: _____

_____

_____

_____

_____

_____

_____

_____

_____

_____

Plotting Pages 25-27

Answers to Questions P-U:

P) _____

Q) _____

R) _____

_____

S) _____

_____

T) _____

_____

U) _____

_____

Main Plot: _____ Plot Variance: _____

Story Outline Form

Characterization

Protagonist's Physical Description: Pages 2,3

Gender: _____ Body Build: _____ Age: _____

Date of Birth: _____ Eye Color: _____ Hair: _____

Write a physical description of your protagonist: _____

_____

_____

Protagonist's Personality: Pages 4-6

First Name: _____ Last Name: _____

Personal Habits 1) _____

Personal Habits 2) _____

Personal Skills: _____

Psychological Traits 1) _____

Psychological Traits 2) _____

Motive: _____

Occupation: _____

Protagonist's Background: Pages 7,19

Birthplace: _____ Grew Up: _____

Type of Dwelling: _____ Soc./Eco. Class: _____

Summarize the personality and background facts: _____

_____

_____

_____

_____

Themes Pages 8,9

Central Theme: _____

Other themes you like: _____

Structure Pages 10,11

Method you want to use to convey the main theme: _____

_____

Primary Character Viewpoint: _____

Time Frame: _____ Story Type: _____

Structure

Continued Pages 11-15

State your Story Question: _____

_____

_____

How will the Story Question be answered: _____

_____

_____

_____

Main Obstacle: _____

Answers to Questions A-C:

A) _____

_____

B) _____

_____

C) _____

_____

Genre: _____ Genre Story Line: _____

Antagonist

D) If the antagonist is not human, what is the antagonist? _____

Antagonist's Physical Description: Pages 2,3

Gender: _____ Body Build: _____ Age: _____

Date of Birth: _____ Eye Color: _____ Hair: _____

Write a physical description of your antagonist: _____

_____

Antagonist's Personality and Background: Pages 4,6,7,17

First Name: _____ Last Name: _____

Personal Habits 1) _____

Personal Habits 2) _____

Personal Skills: _____

Occupation: _____

Birthplace: _____ Grew Up: _____

Type of Dwelling: _____ Soc./Eco. Class: _____

E) Negative Psychological Traits: 1) _____ 2) _____

Example sentence illustrating these traits: _____

_____

_____

Antagonist

F) Human Characteristic: _____

Example sentence illustrating this trait: _____

_____

Summarize these facts about the antagonist to create a character profile: _____

_____

_____

Antagonist's Plan: Pages 17,18

G) State why the antagonist must stop the protagonist:

_____

_____

_____

H) Describe the antagonist's plan: _____

_____

_____

I) The antagonist's relationship to the protagonist is: _____

J) Is the antagonist a flat or round character: _____

Other Characters

Supportive and Secondary Characters: Page 18

The role/relationship of the supportive character to the protagonist is: _____

Is the supportive character flat or round: _____

The role/relationship of the secondary character to the protagonist is: _____

Is the secondary character flat or round: _____

Answers to Questions K-M: Supportive Character

K) _____

_____

L) _____

_____

M) _____

_____

Answers to Questions K-M: Secondary Character

K) _____

_____

L) _____

_____

M) _____

_____

Reproducible

Setting Pages 19-21

The story will take place in: _____ Era: _____

Circle areas you will need to research:

Food   Language   Clothing   Architecture   Currency   Arts   Transportation

Time of Day: _____   Month: _____   Weather: _____

Opening Scene Pages 22-24

Location: _____   Object: _____   Action Verb: _____

Dialogue

N)   The protagonist's character will be revealed by: _____

_____

O)   The opening scene will have the two following characters in conversation: _____

Setting and Opening Scene

Write in sentence format the setting and opening scene for your story by combining all your answers from above: _____

_____

_____

_____

_____

_____

_____

_____

_____

_____

Plotting Pages 25-27

Answers to Questions P-U:

P) _____

Q) _____

R) _____

_____

S) _____

_____

T) _____

_____

U) _____

_____

Main Plot: _____   Plot Variance: _____

Check List

Story Overview:

___ Was your story entertaining?

___ Does your story give the reader an emotional experience?

___ Does the story give the illusion of reality: were you writing primarily in the present tense and letting the reader experience things through the five senses whenever possible?

___ Was there any point in your story where the reader might have wanted to stop reading? If so what can you change?

Protagonist Traits:

___ Are you sure the protagonist was never selfish or showed self-pity?

___ Was your portrayal of the protagonist consistent with his/her character profile?

___ Did you invite trouble wherever you could to help bring out traits?

___ Did you show him/her interacting with animals and objects to show traits?

___ Are traits demonstrated by action and dialogue in at least 3-4 places?

___ Have you relied on behavior to reflect traits? Are they brought out vividly?

___ Highlight the key incidents, quotes or objects of metaphor that stand out to reveal more about the characters.

___ Analyze how the protagonist has grown and changed. Remember as much action as there is so should there be reaction.

Protagonist Goal:

___ Have you convinced the audience that the protagonist's goal is worthwhile? Is it important (not frivolous); is it a specific and universal goal?

___ Have you made it clear as to why it is vital for the protagonist to attain that goal?

___ Does the story pivot around the protagonist achieving that goal?

___ Even if it is a discovery type story did you show the struggle the protagonist had to go through to achieve that goal?

Protagonist Action:

___ Is the protagonist motivated enough? Do actions demonstrate that motivation?

___ Is he/she an active person with a strong drive; a doer with reasons?

___ Did you combine feelings with action and thoughts with action?

___ Is his/her plan of action really full of action?

Theme:

___ Is your theme concise and clearly stated as an assertion?

___ Which method did you use primarily to reveal the theme in your story? Was it the most effective method?

___ How does the theme get to the heart of the matter for the protagonist? Remember the importance of the theme is seeing how it affects the protagonist and watching the reaction.

Viewpoint:

___ Did you include a few direct comments concerning the feelings and thoughts of your viewpoint character?

___ Do you think the reader can identify with the viewpoint character?

Story Question:

___ Did you present a viewpoint character with a goal and or problem?

___ Did your first scene present the story question and contain the onset of the major conflict between the protagonist and antagonist?

___ Does each scene relate to the story question, including the goal or problem for that scene?

___ Did you bring in any secondary story questions which will confuse the audience?

___ Are there any struggles or discussions about things not related to the story question?

Antagonist:

___ What are the antagonist's redeeming characteristics? Is he/she human enough?

___ Does the antagonist have a good reason to be acting as he/she is? They can't be mean without having a good reason.

___ Does the antagonist have a logical plan full of action?

Protagonist and Antagonist:

___ Do you have a feeling about their motives and basic outlook in life?

___ Do you have a concrete image of them? Will your readers?

___ Have you included enough details about their past to make it credible that they want what they want?

___ Highlight where the two have their final confrontation. Is it dramatic?

Secondary Characters:

___ Do all of your characters fulfill their functions of advancing the story?

___ If the protagonist/main character is not sympathetic or likeable, do you have a secondary character who is?

___ It is recommended that one of the secondary characters should have a love interest with or be a confident to the protagonist. Does yours?

Setting:

___ Did you do all the necessary research?

___ Did you mix in symbolism and metaphors?

___ Does each setting provide a good backdrop for each scene and sequel?

___ For each setting, write down how it affects and interacts with the main characters, especially the protagonist, then evaluate it for effectiveness.

Opening Scene:

___ Did you use dramatic action and dialog in the opening scene to catch the attention of the reader?

___ Was the mood and atmosphere in the opening scene compatible with the setting and events and appropriate for the characters?

Dialogue:

___ Do you have lots of dialogue?

___ Did you hear the dialogue out loud? Did it sound like real bits of conversation? Have someone else read it and keep your eyes closed.

___ Overall could you say that most of the dialogue was brief, highly interactive and contained tangible images?

___ Was there enough narrative tension and suspense throughout?

Plotting:

___ Was there continuity in the emotional movement of your story; did it lead to action which caused the resurgence of the story question repeatedly?

___ Did you write your first draft sequentially, without skipping or jumping around between scenes and sequels? In other words, did you follow the plotting chart in chronological order?

Beginning:

___ Did you start as late in your story as possible?

___ Highlight that arresting development which threatened the protagonist's self-concept and equilibrium in the environment. Is it substantial enough so that the reader can identify it?

___ In the beginning scene did you include a physical description of the protagonist? Was the protagonist active and verbal?

___ Did you introduce all the main characters?

Ending:

___ Did you definitely and clearly answer the story question in the end? If you did not it is probably because you strayed from your plotting chart. Try again.

___ Was the ending plausible and logical?

___ Do you think it will surprise and please your readers?

___ What is the ending going to mean to them?

Scenes:

___ How many scenes are there?

___ Do the scenes in the first part of the story help to turn the readers curiosity into anxiety about whether the protagonist will reach his or her goal?

___ Does each scene open with a clearly stated or understood goal for the protagonist?

___ Did the end of each scene answer each scene question?

___ Did each scene end with a disaster that makes the protagonists life more bleak?

___ Did you establish all the threat that you possibly could?

___ Was there substantial conflict in each scene or some kind of serious adversity?
Highlight the complication in each scene and evaluate what the impact will be on the reader. Evaluate whether it's enough to generate sympathy and suspense in the audience for the plight of the protagonist.

___ How are these external conflicts exacerbating the protagonists internal conflicts?

___ Mark with parenthesis the passages that contain exposition, introspection and descriptions. With a different color mark off the passages that contain dialogue and actions. There should

___ be much more of the latter. Could your story be easily turned into a play?

Sequels:

___ How many sequels do you count?

___ Does each sequel investigate not only the feelings but the thoughts of the character involved?

___ Does each sequel have realistic human responses and plausible outcomes?

___ Did you make it obvious as to why a character goes off to do what he/she decides to do?

Check List

Story Overview:

__ Was your story entertaining?

__ Does your story give the reader an emotional experience?

__ Does the story give the illusion of reality: were you writing primarily in the present tense and letting the reader experience things through the five senses whenever possible?

__ Was there any point in your story where the reader might have wanted to stop reading? If so what can you change to make them want to read more?

Protagonist Traits:

__ Are you sure the protagonist was never selfish or showed self-pity?

__ Was your portrayal of the protagonist consistent with his/her character profile?

__ Did you invite trouble wherever you could to help bring out traits?

__ Did you show him/her interacting with animals and objects to show traits?

__ Are traits demonstrated by action and dialogue in at least 3-4 places?

__ Have you relied on behavior to reflect traits? Are they brought out vividly?

__ Highlight the key incidents, quotes or objects of metaphor that stand out to reveal more about the characters.

__ Analyze how the protagonist has grown and changed. Remember as much action as there is so should there be reaction.

Protagonist Goal:

__ Have you convinced the audience that the protagonist's goal is worthwhile? Is it important (not frivolous); is it a specific and universal goal?

__ Have you made it clear as to why it is vital for the protagonist to attain that goal?

__ Does the story pivot around the protagonist achieving that goal?

__ Even if it is a discovery type story did you show the struggle the protagonist had to go through to achieve that goal?

Protagonist Action:

__ Is the protagonist motivated enough? Do actions demonstrate that motivation?

__ Is he/she an active person with a strong drive; a doer with reasons?

__ Did you combine feelings with action and thoughts with action?

__ Is his/her plan of action really full of action?

Theme:

___ Is your theme concise and clearly stated as an assertion?

___ Which method did you use primarily to reveal the theme in your story? Was it the most effective method?

___ How does the theme get to the heart of the matter for the protagonist? The importance of the theme is seeing how it affects the protagonist and watching the reaction.

Viewpoint:

___ Did you include a few direct comments concerning the feelings and thoughts of your viewpoint character?

___ Do you think the reader can identify with the viewpoint character?

Story Question:

___ Did you present a viewpoint character with a goal and or problem?

___ Did your first scene present the story question and contain the onset of the major conflict between the protagonist and antagonist?

___ Does each scene relate to the story question, including the goal or problem for that scene?

___ Did you bring in any secondary story questions which will confuse the audience?

___ Are there any struggles or discussions about things not related to the story question?

Antagonist:

___ What are the antagonist's redeeming characteristics? Is he/she human enough?

___ Does the antagonist have a good reason to be acting as he/she is? They can't be mean without having a good reason.

___ Does the antagonist have a logical plan full of action?

Protagonist and Antagonist:

___ Do you have a feeling about their motives and basic outlook in life?

___ Do you have a concrete image of them? Will your readers?

___ Have you included enough details about their past to make it credible that they want what they want?

___ Highlight where the two have their final confrontation. Is it dramatic?

Secondary Characters:

__ Do all of your characters fulfill their functions of advancing the story?
__ If the protagonist/main character is not sympathetic or likeable, do you have a secondary character who is?
__ It is recommended that one of the secondary characters should have a love interest with or be a confident to the protagonist. Does yours?

Setting:

__ Did you do all the necessary research?
__ Did you mix in symbolism and metaphors?
__ Does each setting provide a good backdrop for each scene and sequel?
__ For each setting, write down how it affects and interacts with the main characters, especially the protagonist, then evaluate it for effectiveness.

Opening Scene:

__ Did you use dramatic action and dialog in the opening scene to catch the attention of the reader?
__ Was the mood and atmosphere in the opening scene compatible with the setting and events and appropriate for the characters?

Dialogue:

__ Do you have lots of dialogue?
__ Did you hear the dialogue out loud? Did it sound like real bits of conversation? Have someone else read it and keep your eyes closed.
__ Overall could you say that most of the dialogue was brief, highly interactive and contained tangible images?
__ Was there enough narrative tension and suspense throughout?

Plotting:

__ Was there continuity in the emotional movement of your story; did it lead to action which caused the resurgence of the story question repeatedly?
__ Did you write your first draft sequentially, without skipping or jumping around between scenes and sequels? In other words, did you follow the plotting chart in chronological order?

Beginning:

___ Did you start as late in your story as possible?
___ Highlight that moment of change, that arresting development which threatened the protagonist's self-concept and equilibrium in the environment. Is it substantial enough so that the reader can identify it?
___ In the beginning scene did you include a physical description of the protagonist? Was the protagonist active and verbal?
___ Did you introduce all the main characters?

Ending:

___ Did you definitely and clearly answer the story question in the end? If you did not it is probably because you strayed from your plotting chart. Try again.
___ Was the ending plausible and logical?
___ Do you think it will surprise and please your readers?
___ What is the ending going to mean to them?

Scenes:

___ How many scenes are there?
___ Do the scenes in the first part of the story help turn the readers curiosity into anxiety about whether the protagonist will reach his or her goal?
___ Does each scene open with a clearly stated or understood goal for the protagonist?
___ Did the end of each scene answer each scene question?
___ Did each scene end with a disaster that makes the protagonists life more bleak?
___ Did you establish all the threat that you possibly could?
___ Was there substantial conflict in each scene or some kind of serious adversity?
    Highlight the complication in each scene and evaluate what the impact will be on the reader. Evaluate whether it's enough to generate sympathy and suspense in the audience for the plight of the protagonist.
___ How are these external conflicts exacerbating the protagonists internal conflicts?
___ Mark with parenthesis the passages that contain exposition, introspection and descriptions. With a different color mark off the passages that contain dialogue and actions. There should be
___ much more of the latter. Could your story be easily turned into a play?

Sequels:

___ How many sequels do you count?
___ Does each sequel investigate not only the feelings but the thoughts of the character involved?
___ Does each sequel have realistic human responses and plausible outcomes?
___ Did you make it obvious as to why a character goes off to do what he/she decides to do?

ORDER FORM

Qty.	Title	Price	Can.Price	Total
	Story Spinner	$19.95	$25.95	
	Spinner Accessory (incl. shipping/handling)	4.00	6.00	
	Subtotal			
	Shipping and Handling (add $3.00 for one book, $1.00 for each additional book)			
	Sales tax (WA residents only, add 8.2%)			
	Total Enclosed			

Telephone Orders:
Call 1-800-468-1994
Have your VISA or
Mastercard ready.

Postal Orders:
Learning Circle Publishing Company
16212 Bothell Way S.E., Ste. F162
Mill Creek, WA 98012-1219

Payment: Please Check One:

❑ Check

❑ VISA®

❑ MasterCard

Expiration Date: _____/_____
Card #: _____
Name on Card: _____
_____

NAME _____

ADDRESS _____

CITY _____

STATE _____ ZIP _____

DAYTIME PHONE _____

Quantity discounts are available.
For more information, call 206-742-2994.

Thank you for your order!

I understand that I may return any books for a full refund if not satisfied.